Succeed In Numeracy

Jeremy Carson, Janet Smith, Janine Frost

illustrations by Jim Hansen

Contents

Introduction

Published by
Arcturus Publishing Limited
for Bookmart Limited
Registered number 2372865
Trading as Bookmart Limited
Desford Road, Enderby,
Leicester LE9 5AD

This edition published 2002

© Arcturus Publishing Limited
1–7 Shand Street, London SE1 2ES

ISBN 1-84193-103-9

Printed and bound in China

Authors: Jeremy Carson,
Janet Smith, Janine Frost
Illustrator: Jim Hansen
Editor: Rebecca Panayiotou
Designer: Susi Martin-Taylor
Cover designer: Alex Ingr

Succeed In Numeracy is a beautifully illustrated and stimulating introduction to mathematics for children in the early years of their formal education.

By the end of Key Stage 1, children should be able to explore and record patterns related to addition, subtraction and multiplication; order sets of numbers and position them on a number line and hundred-square; understand that the position of a digit gives its value; recognise odd and even numbers to 30, and understand the relationship between halving and doubling.

This book looks carefully at these and other main topics of the National Curriculum with the objective of improving your child's understanding, speed and accuracy in mathematics.

How to use this book

- Don't attempt to finish the whole book in one session! Each child is an individual and will have a different concentration span. A topic a day can be taken, or more if the child has the energy.

- Help your child by reading the instructions for them and explaining what is required in the exercises. If they have difficulty with any of the tasks, you can help them.

- Each time your child has completed a page of this book, give them lots of praise and encouragement. Increase their sense of achievement by awarding them a star.

Good luck and good practising!

Numbers to 20

Mrs Manager has washed the football kit. The wind has blown some of the shirts onto the floor.

Which numbers are missing? Write them in the boxes below.

Mr Manager has to collect the shirts for the match, but the numbers have come off in the wash. Can you write them back on for him?

Well done! Award yourself a star!

The Same, More, or Fewer?

Diver Dave has gone swimming under the sea. He has found lots of sea life. He has even spotted a huge sea serpent!

How many dolphins did he see? ☐

How many shells did he see? ☐

So did he see **more** shells or **more** dolphins? _____

How many fish did he see? ☐

How many starfish did he see? ☐

So did he see **fewer** fish or **fewer** starfish? _____

How many crabs did he see? ☐

What two things did he see the **same** amount of? Circle the correct pictures.

How many sea life characters did Diver Dave see altogether? ☐

Well done! Award yourself a star!

When Diver Dave came back to the top of the ocean he saw a huge sea serpent. It had lots of fins on its back. Some of them have numbers on them. Can you fill in the missing numbers?

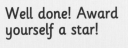

Well done! Award yourself a star!

Number Bonds with Jungle Jane

Jungle Jane has gone exploring. On her travels, she has found some spotty snakes. We are going to help Jane find pairs of numbers that make 10.

Colour in the blank spots of the snakes to find out how many more make 10.

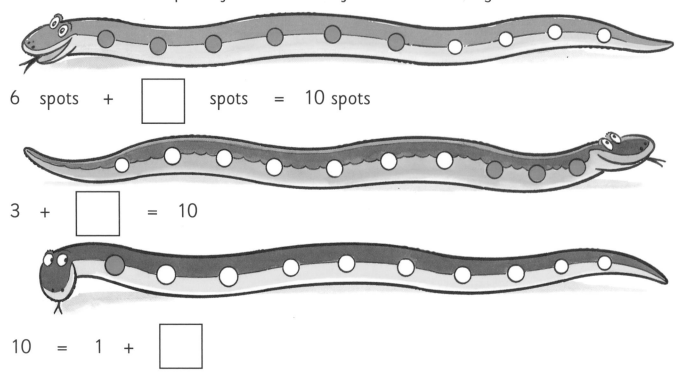

6   spots   +   ☐   spots   =   10 spots

3   +   ☐   =   10

10   =   1   +   ☐

Colour each snake's spots with two different colours to find your own pairs of numbers that make 10. Record your answers underneath.

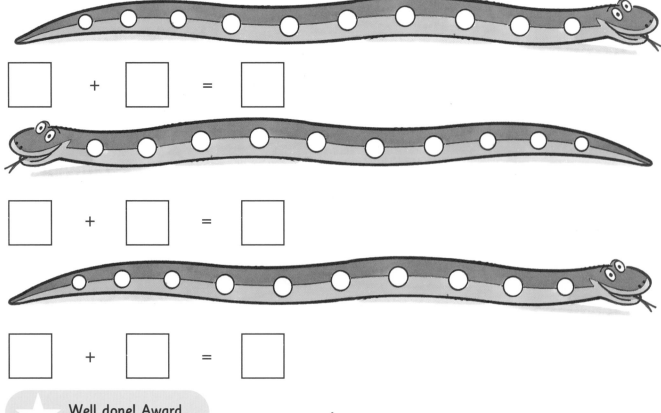

☐   +   ☐   =   ☐

☐   +   ☐   =   ☐

☐   +   ☐   =   ☐

6

Jane has noticed something interesting about numbers that add up to 10.
Cheery Chimp will show you her ideas with his bananas.

The numbers can be swapped around!

If   6   +   4   =   10

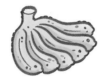

Then   4   +   6   =   10   as well!

Use these 10 bananas to help you!

Can you help Jane finish her notes?

If   3 + 7 = 10

Then   7 + ☐ = 10

If   8 + 2 = 10

Then   ☐ + 8 = 10

If   1 + 9 = 10

Then   9 + ☐ = 10

If   6 + 4 = 10

Then   4 + ☐ = 10

Well done! Award yourself a star!

Taking Away Wriggly Worms!

Hold up your hand and wriggle your fingers. They are 5 wriggly worms! Now make your other hand into a hungry bird. It's going to eat the worms!

There are 5 worms. If the bird eats 1 worm how many are left?

Count your fingers that are left. There are 4. The bird has **taken away** 1 worm. We say: 5 **take away** 1 = 4.

There is a special sign for take away: —

—	means	**take away**
	or	**subtract**
	or	**minus**
	or	**less than**

5 take away 1 = 4   5 subtract 1 = 4   5 minus 1 = 4

1 less than 5 = 4   5 - 1 = 4

Now use your 5 wriggly worms to do these sums:

If the bird eats 3 worms how many are left?   5 - 3 = ☐

If the bird eats 4 worms how many are left?   5 - 4 = ☐

If the bird eats 5 worms how many are left?   5 - ☐ = ☐

If the bird eats no worms how many are left?   5 - ☐ = ☐

How many worms does the bird need to eat for 3 to be left? 5 - ☐ = 3

Now hold up **all** your fingers.

How many do you have altogether?

Fold down 5 fingers.
How many do you have left?

10 - 5 = ☐

Can you use your fingers to help you with these questions?

10 - 3 = ☐   10 - 2 = ☐

10 - 7 = ☐   10 - 9 = ☐

Now try these:

10 - ☐ = 6   10 - ☐ = 2

10 - ☐ = 0   10 - ☐ = 9

Now write two number sentences of your own!

10 - ☐ = ☐   10 - ☐ = ☐

Parent tip:
Demonstrate subtraction using practical items like sweets, pasta shapes or counters. This makes it easier for children to grasp the concept. Encourage reference to all ten fingers too - after all, they're a portable calculator!

Well done! Award yourself a star!

Odds, Evens, and Seeing Double!

Here is a number line. The red numbers in the snake are **odd** numbers. The yellow numbers in the snake are **even** numbers. Look at these examples:

We can see that these numbers are odd: | 1 | 17 | 29 |

We can see that these numbers are even: | 2 | 10 | 26 |

Write down the odd numbers here:

Write down the even numbers here:

Jake has 12 counters. To check if 12 is an even number, Jake lays them out in sets of two:

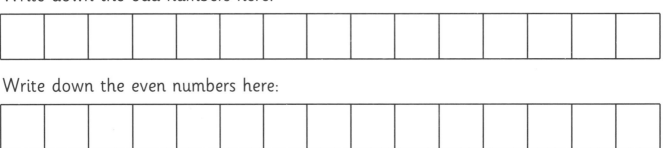

Each counter has a partner which proves that 12 is an **even** number.

Jess has 13 counters. She lays them out in sets of two:

One of her counters does **not** have a partner, so she knows that 13 is an **odd** number.

Well done! Award yourself a star!

10

Kim and Kirsty are identical twins!

Kim has 2 pigtails. So does Kirsty. Together, they have 4 pigtails, or **double** 2.

Can you use doubling to answer these questions?

How many socks do Kim and Kirsty have altogether?

2 + 2 = ☐   or double 2 = ☐

How many freckles do Kim and Kirsty have altogether?

☐ + ☐ = ☐ or double ☐ = ☐

How many buttons do Kim and Kirsty have altogether?

☐ + ☐ = ☐ or double ☐ = ☐

How many flowers on their skirts altogether?

☐ + ☐ = ☐ or double ☐ = ☐

How many fingers and thumbs altogether?

☐ + ☐ = ☐ or double ☐ = ☐

What other doubles can you find?

11

Rocket Maths

Out in space, some rockets are practising making numbers. Can you see how they do it?

Rocket 10 is chasing Rocket 2!

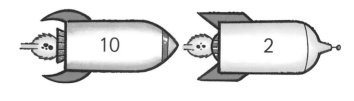

When they meet they make 12!

Can you see how the 10 joins with the 2 to make the number 12? The zero is now hidden behind the 2!

What number will these two rockets make?

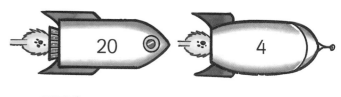

They will make 24!

What numbers will these rockets make?

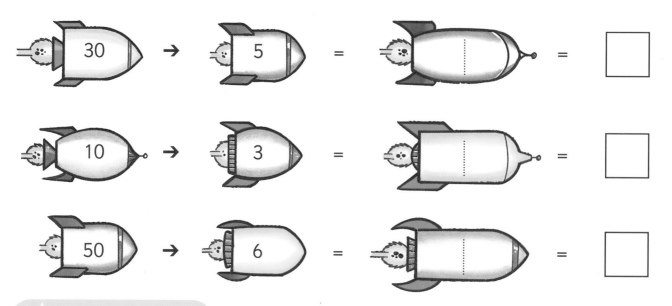

Well done! Award yourself a star!

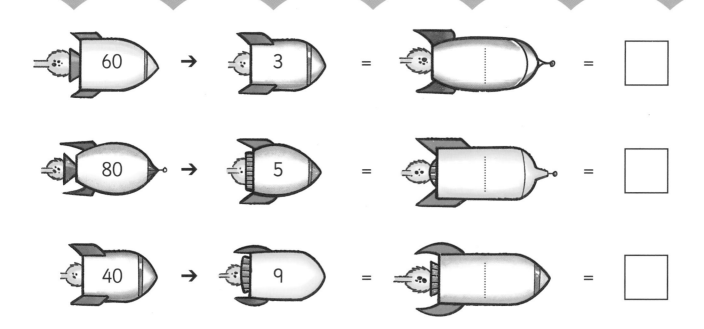

Can you say which rockets made these numbers?

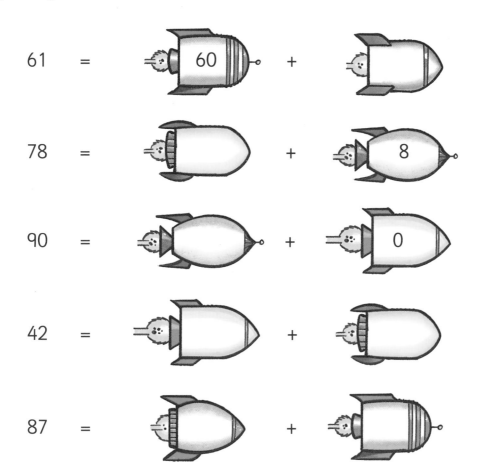

61 = 60 +

78 = + 8

90 = + 0

42 = +

87 = +

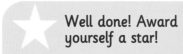

Well done! Award yourself a star!

Adventures in the Lift!

We are in the lift of the **Humpty Hotel**! Look at this set of buttons. The buttons for some floors have been pressed so many times that the numbers have rubbed off.

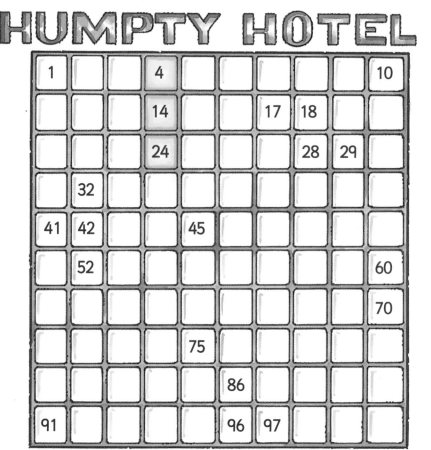

HUMPTY HOTEL

1			4						10
			14			17	18		
			24				28	29	
	32								
41	42			45					
	52								60
									70
				75					
					86				
91					96	97			

Can you fill in the missing numbers? How did you know what they were?

Toby the Teaman is on floor 4. He presses the button for floor 14.

How many floors up did he go?

Next, he presses the button for floor 24. How many floors up does he go now?

Which button do you think he will press to go up another 10 floors?

Did you spot the pattern? To move on 10 more, you just need to press the button underneath – you don't need to press all the buttons in between!

Parent tip:
Being able to count in 10s from a given number will help your child with their mental calculation strategies. For example, 36 + 21 can be done by adding 20 to 36, then adding 1.

Can you complete these patterns for adding or subtracting 10? Use the buttons to help you.

21,   31,   41,   51, ☐ , ☐ , ☐

35,   45, ☐ , ☐ ,   75,   85, ☐

88,   78,   68, ☐ , ☐ , ☐ , 28

Can you help the hotel manager? He can't find his staff.

Can you work out which floors they're on? Use the lift control panel to help you.

Colin the Cleaner was on floor 16.
He went up 20 floors. What floor is he on now?

16 + 20 = ☐   So he is on floor _____

Maggie the Maid was on floor 38.
She went up 40 floors. What floor is she on now?

38 + 40 = ☐   So she is on floor _____

Bertie the Bed Maker was on floor 93.
He went down 30 floors. What floor is he on now?

93 - 30 = ☐   So he is on floor _____

Charlie the Chef was on floor 72.
He went down 50 floors. What floor is he on now?

72 - 50 = ☐   So he is on floor _____

Well done! Award
yourself a star!

Planet Problems

King Digit lives on the planet **Number**. He has called together all his subjects from the surrounding planets. Can you help him work out how many visitors he has? The number on each rocket tells you how many aliens are inside.

These two rockets have arrived:

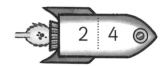 and

First, let's split these rockets up!

 + and

Let's add the tens first:

Now we can add the units:

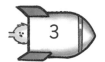

We now have:

If we put these rockets together, they make:

Try these in the same way: 2 | 4 and 1 | 1

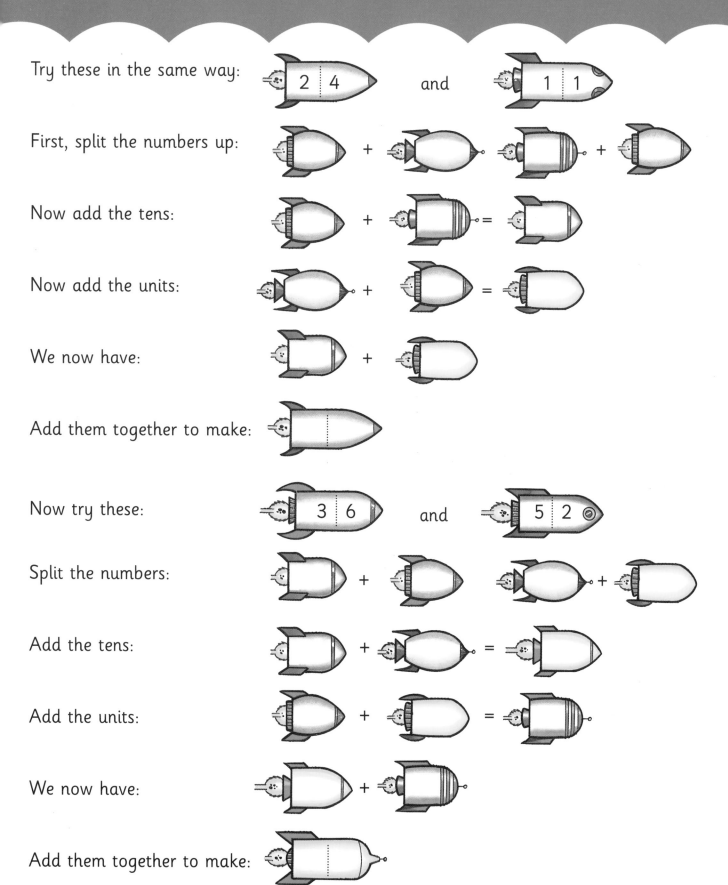

First, split the numbers up: + | +

Now add the tens: + =

Now add the units: + =

We now have: +

Add them together to make:

Now try these: 3 | 6 and 5 | 2

Split the numbers: + | +

Add the tens: + =

Add the units: + =

We now have: +

Add them together to make:

Well done! Award yourself a star!

Let's Go Shopping!

Stan and Kitty are going shopping. They are going to their favourite toy shop! Let's see how much pocket money they have.

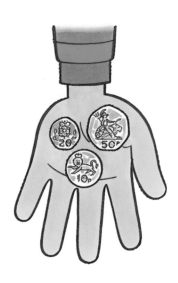

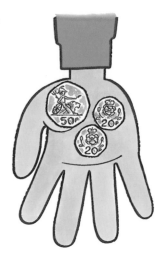

Stan has:

Kitty has:

☐ p + ☐ p + ☐ p = ☐ p   ☐ p + ☐ p + ☐ p = ☐ p

Dad gives Stan five more coins. Here they are:

     = ☐ p

How much does he have now altogether?

☐ p + ☐ p = ☐ p

Kitty spends 20p on a comic. How much money does she have left?

☐ p - ☐20☐ p = ☐ p

Well done! Award yourself a star!

Parent tip:
Experimenting with money is an excellent way of practising addition, subtraction and counting with your child. Encourage them to play with coins and to notice prices when out shopping.

Now Stan and Kitty are in the shop. There is plenty to buy:

You have worked out how much money Stan and Kitty now have. Look at all the goodies in the shop. They can't decide what to spend their money on. Can you find two different ways each of them could spend **all** of it?

For example, Stan could buy:
a comic, a tub of paint, and a number book.   20p + 30p + 40p = 90p

Stan:

1. _____

2. _____

Kitty:

1. _____

2. _____

Could Kitty buy two pens and a ball with her money?   Yes ☐   No ☐

Could Stan buy three stickers and a toy car?   Yes ☐   No ☐

Could you buy a bucket and a spade with £1.50?   Yes ☐   No ☐

What is the cheapest item in the shop?   _____

What are the most expensive items in the shop?   _____

19

Well done! Award yourself a star!

Wholes, Halves, and Quarters

It's tea time! Kim and Kirsty are waiting for their dinner: one **whole** pizza.

The twins are very hungry. They both want some pizza. We can make it fair by cutting the pizza into two parts that are the same. The parts are equal. Each of the parts is called a **half**.

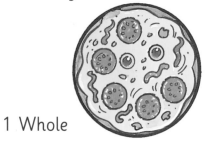

1 Whole

2 Halves

> **2** halves make **1** whole.   **1** whole can be split into **2** halves.
>
> There is a special sign for a half. It looks like this: $^1/_2$

It is not only single objects that can be halved. Groups of things can also be halved. For example:

I have 10 sweets.

I give 5 to my friend.

5 is half of 10. Therefore, I have given half of my sweets to my friend.

Use your fingers to help you decide:

What is $^1/_2$ of 8? ☐

What is $^1/_2$ of 6? ☐

What is $^1/_2$ of 4? ☐

Well done! Award yourself a star!

20

Parent tip:
A half is a fundamental part of maths and is actually quite an easy concept to grasp, especially if real items like foodstuffs, counters, coins or beads are used. When your child is ready, introduce the notion of halving odd numbers, leaving a half 'over', e.g., half of 7 is 3 $^1/_2$.

Now it's time for dessert! Kim and Kirsty have baked themselves a cake. They want to give some to their mum and dad as well. That makes 4 people altogether. They cut the cake into 4 equal pieces. Each of these pieces is called a **quarter**.

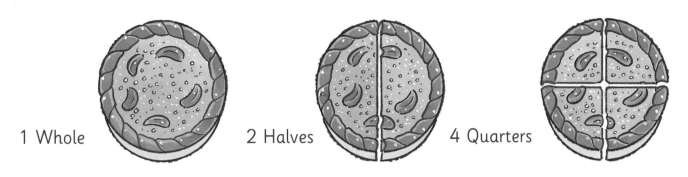

1 Whole   2 Halves   4 Quarters

4 quarters make **1** whole.   **1** whole can be split into **4** quarters.

There is a special sign for a quarter. It is: $^1/4$

Look at these pictures. Fill in the boxes with either 1, $^1/2$ or $^1/4$ to show whether the coloured area represents a whole, a half or a quarter.

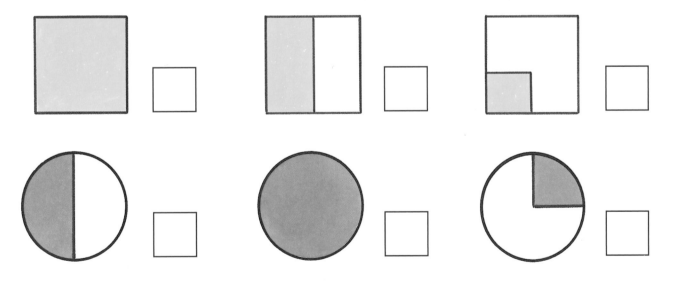

Now shade these pictures to show the fraction:

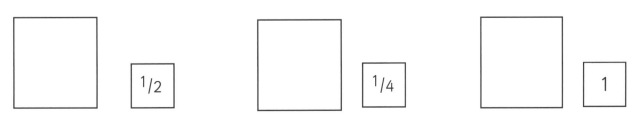

$^1/2$ $^1/4$ 1

Well done! Award
yourself a star!

Magic Multiplication

Alfie has made a potato print. He has printed 5 pieces of paper with 2 big red dots. Now he puts them in a row to add them up.

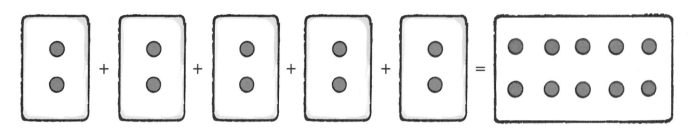

When he adds up his 5 lots of 2 he finds it makes 10.
We say: 5 **lots of** 2 make 10.

We have a special sign for lots of: **x**

	means	**lots of**
x	or	**multiplied by**
	or	**times**

5 lots of 2 = 10   5 multiplied by 2 = 10   5 times 2 = 10

5 x 2 = 10

Can you do these sums?

1 x 2 = ☐   2 x 2 = ☐   3 x 2 = ☐

4 x 2 = ☐   5 x 2 = ☐   6 x 2 = ☐

7 x 2 = ☐   8 x 2 = ☐   9 x 2 = ☐

10 x 2 = ☐

Well done! Award yourself a star!

Step into the **Fun Times** sweet shop! Mr Sweet lives in the shop and wants to know how many sweets he has. Can you help him?

Look at these 4 bags of sweets. Each bag has 5 sweets in it.

4 lots of 5 sweets = 20 sweets altogether.   4 x 5 = 20

Now try the following sums. Use the sweet bags to help you.

1 x 5 = ☐   2 x 5 = ☐   3 x 5 = ☐

4 x 5 = ☐   5 x 5 = ☐   6 x 5 = ☐

7 x 5 = ☐   8 x 5 = ☐   9 x 5 = ☐

                                       10 x 5 = ☐

Parent tip:
Children in Key Stage 1 need to know their 2, 5 and 10 times tables. Try to make learning these fun, using practical objects to count and group. Children can practise by writing tables, chanting tables and looking for quick ways to remember the facts, e.g., 2 x 5 is the same as 5 x 2 - you don't need to learn both!

23

Well done! Award yourself a star!

Fabulous Function Machines

Now it's time for you to have fun with what you have learnt!

You can choose any number you like and place it into the function machine.
Can you work out what will come out the other side?

| □ | → | +10 | → | □ | | □ | → | -30 | → | □ |

| □ | → | x 2 | → | □ | | □ | → | x10 | → | □ |

| □ | → | x 5 | → | □ | | □ | → | +23 | → | □ |

| □ | → | +2 | → | □ | | □ | → | -6 | → | □ |

Now write your own functions!

| 6 | → | □ | → | □ | | □ | → | □ | → | □ |

| 11 | → | □ | → | □ | | □ | → | □ | → | □ |

| 51 | → | □ | → | □ | | □ | → | □ | → | □ |

| 2 | → | □ | → | □ | | □ | → | □ | → | □ |